SPACE
to space and back
on the shuttle
TRAVELER

by BETTY POLISAR REIGOT

SCHOLASTIC INC.
New York Toronto London Auckland Sydney Tokyo

For Bob and Ira
     my brothers and fellow travelers
        in time and space...

Acknowledgment

The cooperation and generous assistance of the people at NASA's Johnson Space Center is deeply appreciated. Special thanks to Frank Hughes of the Crew Training Division, Flight Operations for giving us the benefit of his expertise.

Photographs courtesy of the
National Aeronautics and Space Administration

Illustrations by Ted Hanke

ISBN 0-590-32841-7

12 11 10 9 8 7 6 5 4 3 2 1   9   3 4 5 6 7/8
                          Printed in the U.S.A.   09

Contents

The shuttle is ready at Kennedy Space Center. Its nose points to the sky. Would you like to be a space traveler on the shuttle and rocket into space?

Two communications satellites are on board the shuttle for this flight. They will be left in space to orbit Earth for many years. You will be home again in five days.

The shuttle will soar 320 kilometers (200 miles) above Earth, where it will orbit this planet. You will reach orbit in less than 10 minutes! Traveling that distance by car takes 5 hours or more.

Many years of work and planning have made a space trip like this possible. Now, space traveler, it is time to go!

The Shuttle

There are three parts to the shuttle:
the *orbiter;*
the huge, red *external fuel tank;*
two long, white *rocket boosters.*
The orbiter is like a delivery truck. It can deliver things to space, bring objects back to Earth, and make it possible to repair some objects already in space.

The tank and the rocket boosters supply the power to get the orbiter into space. Once the orbiter is under way, the boosters, and then the tank, will separate from it.

The shuttle, with its three parts secured to one another, now sits on the launch pad, waiting for lift-off.

The shuttle is moved slowly out of the Vehicle Assembly Building at Kennedy Space Center, on its way to the launch pad.

The Flight Crew

You can be the *commander* on the shuttle flight.

You will be in charge. There will be four other crew members besides you. They are:

The pilot—Like you, the pilot is a trained astronaut who knows how to fly aircraft and spacecraft. The pilot will assist you in flying the shuttle out to space and back.

Two mission specialists—These crew members are also astronauts. One of them aids the pilot. The other is in charge of carrying out the flight's main purpose and any other jobs scheduled for that flight.

The payload specialist—This person may not be an astronaut, but he or she is an expert about the cargo hauled by the shuttle. Not all flights include a payload specialist. Yours does because the cargo you are taking into space needs one.

The cargo is called a payload because somebody pays to have it carried into space. It is placed in a large section of the orbiter called the *payload bay*, or *cargo bay*.

The payload on your flight is two communications satellites. The payload specialist in your crew is a communications engineer.

The main purpose of your mission will be to deploy the satellites into space. Once they are in orbit, the communications satellites will transmit, or relay, messages easily to many parts of Earth.

These two astronauts are in a simulator, where they can practice everything they will have to do in a real flight. The commander is on the left, the pilot on the right.

Different missions will take different payloads. Sometimes several experts will be on board. They may be engineers; technicians; doctors; or scientists such as astronomers, biologists, or meteorologists. Some missions will have several different kinds of experts.

The orbiter can carry up to seven people. The basic crew is always the commander, the pilot, and the two mission specialists.

Shuttle flights may be as long as 30 days. Your flight will take just 5 days.

Because you're the commander, you make the decisions during the flight. You will try for total success. But something may happen that you don't expect. You may decide at any time that the plans must be changed. Or you may not be able to do all that is planned. Always, the safety of the crew comes first.

Of course, you'll have a lot of help—from crew members; the computers on board; Mission Control at Johnson Space Center in Houston, Texas; and from different stations around the globe that can relay messages from you to Mission Control.

Throughout your flight, monitors on the ground at Johnson Space Center pay close attention to how things are going. They are ready for messages from you. They watch your progress on computer consoles as you go up, circle Earth for days, and then come down. They even check each crew member's health.

The people on the ground who are trained in space technology—computer science, aerodynamics (AIR-O-DIE-NAM-ICS), engineering, medicine, rocket engines, and so on—are as important to the Space Transportation System as the astronauts.

Flight directors at the control centers will direct a team of people who give you important information and data. These people will help you solve any problems that arise. And they will arrange for another place for you to land, if you need it.

You've spent at least one year getting special training just in space flight. You have learned many things. You will have a lot to do, and you know what you need to know to be commander of a shuttle flight.

The Countdown

The final countdown begins five hours before lift-off. The *ground crew* comes aboard to make sure everything works properly, and then they leave.

Two hours before lift-off, you and the other members of the *flight crew* board the shuttle. You crawl through a round opening—the side hatch—and stand on the wall! (The wall is the floor when the shuttle is pointed upward.)

The commander's seat is always on the left, the pilot's on the right. The mission specialists sit behind the pilot.

Grab a handle here, another one there, to help you climb up to the flight deck. That's where all the instruments and windows are.

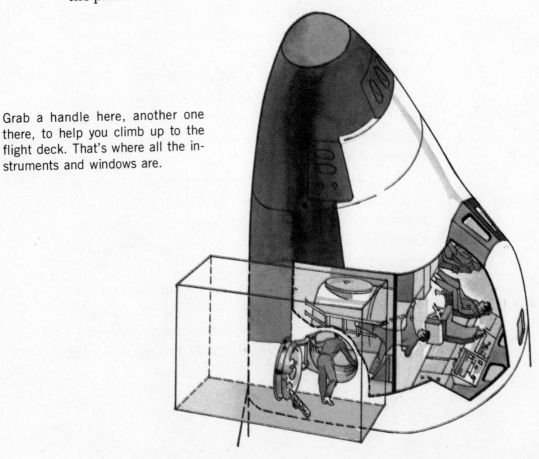

There isn't much room. Only four seats fit on the flight deck. Payload specialists usually sit in the area below the flight deck.

You climb into your seat and buckle up. Have you ever lain on your bed, or on the floor, with your knees bent and your feet on the wall? That's your position when you lift off in the shuttle.

The countdown continues:

1 (hour): 45 (minutes): 20 (seconds)

1:45:19

1:45:18

Time goes fast. Each operation must be done in exact order at the exact time. Split seconds can matter greatly in the course of a shuttle flight. The right timing puts the shuttle in the proper orbit, prevents bad accidents, and can make the difference between any part of the flight going right or wrong.

Instruments and computers at Kennedy Launch Control, at Johnson Mission Control, and those in the flight deck of the orbiter—where you are now—are all connected.

You and the flight controllers in the control centers communicate back and forth with each other. There are many details. The mission specialists read the checklists to you and the pilot. Nothing must be forgotten.

Moments before lift-off, the on-board computers are loaded with programs needed for the launch. They perform the final countdown automatically. They trigger the right operation at the right second in lightning speed.

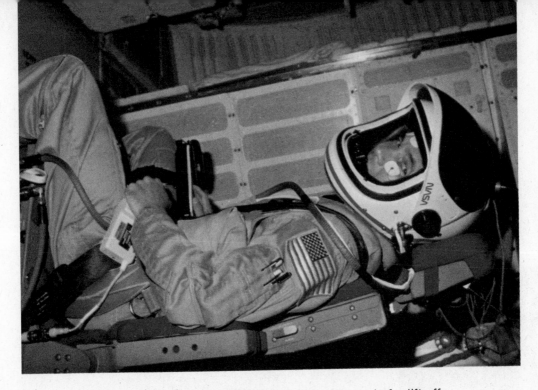

The mission specialist buckles into his seat, ready for lift-off.

About six seconds before zero countdown, the orbiter's main engines start up. Fuel from the big external tank pours through feed lines that are as wide as a circle you make with your arms. Fuel powers the three engines in the tail of the orbiter.

The two rocket boosters—each longer than a convoy of four gasoline trucks—begin firing. All five engines are now at full blast.

The ground trembles. The big hulk of the shuttle pushes upward in a tremendous thrust. White light from the firing engines streams from the tail of the shuttle and great clouds of smoke billow out all over the ground.

The Ascent

You can feel the power of the engines. They drive the shuttle against the pull of Earth's gravity—the force that pulls all things down on Earth.

Look out the side windows. Swiftly, the ground seems to fall away.

The shuttle clears the service tower of the launch pad and angles off into space. In a gentle roll, the external tank and the rocket boosters are now on top. The orbiter is upside down. So are you.

This allows you to see the earth and check that you are heading in the correct direction. If you flew heads up, you couldn't see the earth because the tank would block your view.

Before you escape Earth's strong gravity, the force of the engines becomes three times as great. You are three times as heavy. Scientists call this 3-G. A stronger pull would be uncomfortable.

In less than a minute you're moving at the same speed as sound—called Mach (MOC) One.

A minute later, you are 50 kilometers (30 miles) up and flying four-and-a-half times faster than sound, or Mach 4.5.

This may give you an idea of the speed of sound: Imagine you are in the back of a large auditorium. The band on the stage plays their last note and you hear it a fraction of a second after the band has stopped playing. That's how fast the sound travels to the back of the auditorium!

The rocket-booster casings are towed back to Cape Canaveral where they are cleaned and filled again for another mission.

The two rocket boosters are used up. By remote control, they are separated from the shuttle. Their empty casings float down, by parachutes, and drop gently into the ocean. Ships wait to tow them back to dry land to be reloaded and used again many times.

The external tank (ET), still attached, continues to pour fuel into the main engines of the orbiter. Your speed is now up to Mach 15.

Eight minutes after lift-off, the ET is almost empty. The orbiter's main engines cut off at Mach 26. The spacecraft now separates itself from the ET.

As the tank falls down and away, it breaks apart. Most of the pieces change to vapor. Any remaining pieces usually end up in the Indian Ocean. A new tank will be built for the next shuttle flight.

You coast briefly in silent space. Then you fire two small on-board engines. These engines shoot the orbiter away from the ET and farther out in space, putting it into its first orbit—only ten minutes after leaving the ground.

You fire the engines again about 30 minutes later to complete the job. This second firing puts the shuttle in the orbit you wish to be in for this flight.

You have taken the shuttle through a very difficult stage.

Now that you are in orbit, the first thing you must do is to open the cargo bay doors. This lets out all the heat collected during the ascent that would interfere with your flight.

The doors of the cargo bay stay open while the ship is in orbit. The cargo bay is a little bigger than a tour bus and can carry many different objects of different sizes.

Living in Space

The orbiter is now traveling more than 28,000 kilometers (17,500 miles) per hour. At that speed you could get from sea level to the top of Earth's highest mountains in one second!

How high are you? You're 320 kilometers (200 miles) above the surface of the earth. Even though you are so far away, you're still held back by Earth's gravity.

You cannot feel the pull, but it's enough to keep you in place. Scientists call this microgravity.

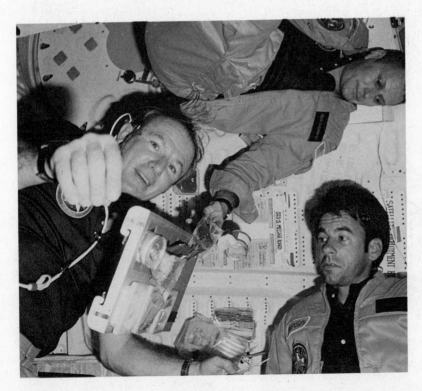

People inside the orbiter float freely in microgravity.

15

Because of its speed, the orbiter doesn't fall down. Because of Earth's gravity, the orbiter doesn't fly off deeper into space. Instead, you move in a circle called an orbit.

Around Earth you spin. You will have sunlight for 45 minutes as you fly between the sun and Earth. The next 45 minutes will be dark because Earth will block the sun's rays. Then there is another sunrise.

For the next five days you will live and work in space. Living in space is very different from living on Earth. You must know how to live in space before you can do any work there.

The cabin—There are three levels to the cabin. The upper level is the flight deck. That is your work place. The seats used by the specialists are stowed while you are in space.

The mid-deck is your home in space. It's where

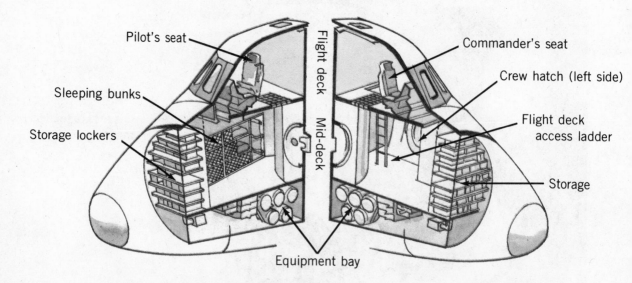

Pilot's seat

Commander's seat

Crew hatch (left side)

Sleeping bunks

Storage lockers

Flight deck access ladder

Storage

Flight deck

Mid-deck

Equipment bay

you eat, sleep, wash, read, write, or just relax. You may want to have a book, or a diary, or perhaps a camera on your trip.

There is a galley for preparing meals, a bathroom, and lockers for your clothes and personal belongings.

Some experiments are also performed on the middeck. To get from one deck to another, you just float up or down one of the two hatchways.

There is a level beneath your space home which provides room for pipes, ducts, fans, containers, and other equipment.

This equipment makes living in space possible. It maintains atmosphere and pressure in the orbiter much like we have on Earth. It removes the poisonous carbon dioxide you exhale. It filters the air, removes dirt and dust, and does various other housecleaning jobs.

Gases, such as nitrogen, oxygen, and hydrogen, are taken up in containers. These gases are combined to provide the proper mix of air to breathe and to make water for washing and drinking.

When humans go up in space, they must bring with them what they need to stay alive.

Weightlessness—In microgravity, everything is almost as light as a feather. That doesn't mean you

This drawing is called a "cutaway." The nose of the orbiter has been "cut" right down the middle and spread apart to show the three levels of the orbiter cabin.

can take a deep breath and blow another person across the cabin. But things tend to float around if they are not held down in some way.

Just a touch against the wall may send you over to the other side. Trying to fix something on the floor may set you off doing one somersault after another.

Being weightless can be a lot of fun—but it presents certain problems. Engineers, technicians, and scientists have tried to come up with solutions. Some of them work and some don't. We have no way to create a microgravity environment on Earth. So a lot of the solutions to overcome weightlessness can be tested only in space.

Your body undergoes changes in microgravity. Without the pull downward, you become 2½–5 centimeters (1–2 inches) taller than on Earth.

We cannot create a microgravitiy environment on Earth—but going under water comes close to it. This astronaut is testing the communication system in his spacesuit in a water tank at Johnson Space Center.

This is your normal posture on Earth.

This is your posture in space. Your body bends slightly at the waist, hips and knees. Your arms float out in front of you unless you pull them back.

Your posture is different. When you sit, your body leans backward. Your toes point so you can't stand straight with your feet flat.

The blood inside your body shifts from being mostly in the lower part and spreads upward more. Your feet are narrower. Your waist is smaller. Your face is fuller.

Since the inside of the body is as weightless as the outside, some astronauts have trouble keeping food down. A burp can make your food come up. Scientists are trying to solve this problem, too.

Your flight suit on board is lightweight, comfortable, and fireproof. It has lots of pockets all over. They hold small items that would otherwise float around—such as your pen, pencil, data book, glasses, pocket knife, and a pair of scissors.

Eating—There is a great variety of food. On your five-day mission, different meals are planned for every day. The food keeps fresh without a refrigerator or freezer.

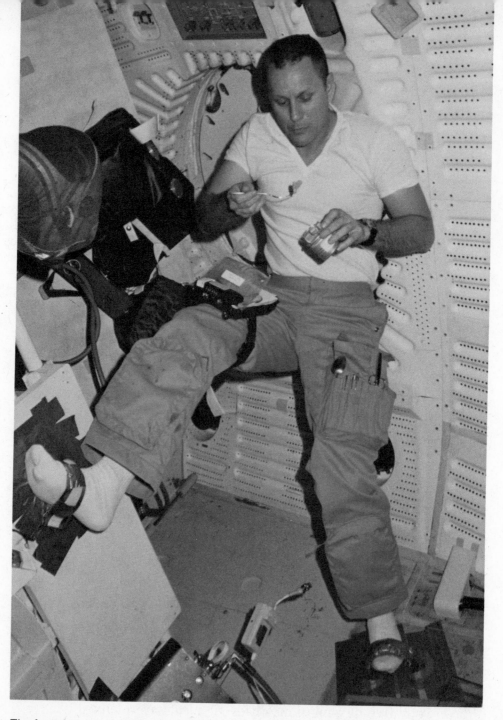

The foot straps help to keep the astronaut anchored down while he eats. If he didn't hold onto his food and fork, they would float away! His tools are safely tucked away in the many pockets of his pants.

All around the orbiter are strips of Velcro — a material things stick to. A flashlight, a pencil, a comb, or any other small object will stay put against the Velcro until you need it.

Some foods need water added first. Others should be heated. And still others don't need anything but to be eaten.

You can have applesauce, hamburger, chicken and noodles, cookies, scrambled eggs, nuts, fruits, vegetables, puddings, peanut butter, soups, macaroni and cheese, strawberries, snacks and candy, and lots more.

You can sip lemonade, apple juice, hot chocolate, coffee, tea, punch, and other drinks. No soda! It makes you burp.

Bread must be soft. Crusty bread gets crumby, and crumbs float around. Salt, pepper, and sugar grains would float around, too. So they are used in liquid form. There is also ketchup, mustard, and mayonnaise.

Keeping clean—Each member of the crew has a personal hygiene kit. It's for your toothbrush, toothpaste, nail clippers, soap, comb, brush, skin lotion, deodorant, and so on.

At the personal hygiene station there is a mirror, a light, and a place to wash. You can draw a curtain across to give you privacy.

There is no shower. You bathe your entire body with a washcloth and dry off with a towel. You and the others each have your own supply of washcloths and towels.

When you use the toilet, you attach a seat belt and use the footrests. There is a light to read by. You can even look through the side hatch to see outside.

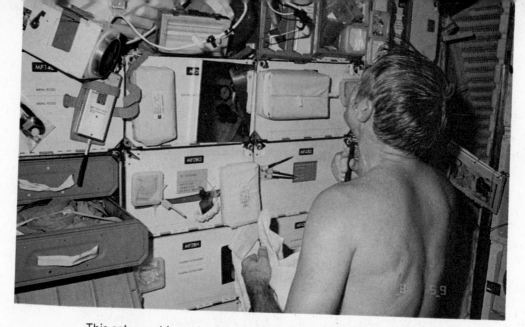

This astronaut has what he needs to shave — a mirror, a light, and some water nearby.

A hand-washing device keeps water from floating around the cabin.

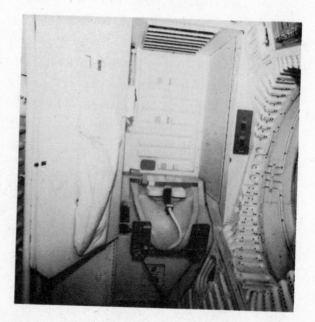

Each crew member has a supply of towels in his or her own color so they don't get mixed up. Used towels go in a trash bag on the door near the toilet.

Liquid waste from washing and urinating flows into a container. When that fills up it is dumped overboard. Solid wastes go into a separate compartment where they are dried up and disposed of after landing.

Sleeping—There are four sleep bunks on the orbiter. Each bunk has a padded board, a sleeping bag, a curtain for privacy, and a small light.

You climb into your sleeping bag. Zip up, with your arms outside. A sling or belt keeps you pressed gently against the board so you feel as though you're lying on a bed.

Some astronauts are not comfortable this way. They simply go to a corner and float off somewhere to sleep. Some end up resting against the ceiling.

If the cabin light bothers you, you can wear a mask. If the noise is too loud, you can use earplugs.

When everyone sleeps at the same time, one must wear a radio headset. Someone must receive any emergency messages from ground control. If seven people are on a mission, they will sleep in shifts.

Every crew member may take a few personal items on the flight. This astronaut enjoys a book while resting in his bunk.

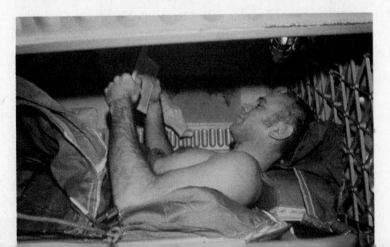

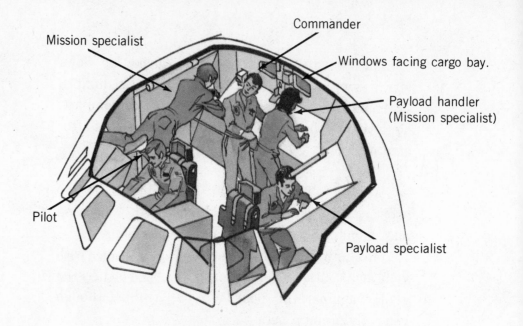

Mission specialist

Commander

Windows facing cargo bay.

Payload handler
(Mission specialist)

Pilot

Payload specialist

Working in Space

Now that your flight has reached orbit stage, and the crew has what it needs to live in space, you can all get to work.

The mission and payload specialists have been passengers so far. Now their jobs begin. In fact, all the crew members have a special task once the ship is in orbit.

The work station—The crew works at the back of the flight deck, called the *aft flight deck*. It's a U-shaped area that has instruments and controls to carry out the mission.

What the crew does—As commander, you work at the left window overlooking the cargo bay. Your job is to maneuver the orbiter.

By using the controls in front of you in the right combination, you can change the orbiter's position or its course. You can also bring the orbiter close to another object in space or dock it with another spacecraft—though you won't have to do that during this mission.

The pilot remains in his seat in order to help control the orbiter. A mission specialist, standing before the right window, is now the payload handler. He or she operates a long mechanical arm—called the Remote Manipulator Arm—that is attached to the side of the cargo bay. One of the jobs of this mission is to find out how well the arm works and to practice using it.

From the work station, the payload specialist checks the payload in the cargo bay to see that it

These drawings show the mechanical arm at work. At the left, the arm is lifting a satellite up from the cargo bay. On the right, it is preparing to launch the satellite into orbit.

The arm, which has a shoulder, elbow, and wrist, like our arm, can also reach up and pull objects out of space. This helpful Remote Manipulator Arm was made in Canada.

works properly. The payload on this flight is two communications satellites. The most important goal of the flight is to deploy, or send out, in space the two communications satellites.

Just as you, the commander, are in charge of the overall flight, one mission specialist is in charge of the payload deploy portion of the mission. This mission specialist uses another set of computer terminals and spacecraft systems to check out the satellites and determine when and where to launch them. He or she also floats around taking as many photographs as possible. The photographs are used as a record of this flight and help to plan future missions.

The crew works closely together to complete the tasks of the mission. You and the others each do a part of the whole job. All of you do your best to make sure there are no slip-ups and no accidents.

Carrying out the mission—To deploy the two communications satellites, one satellite will be released first. The next day, the second one will be sent out in space, too.

After the satellite moves out of the cargo bay and is a safe distance from the orbiter, the satellite automatically fires a rocket engine. That engine shoots the satellite up to almost 36,000 kilometers (22,300 miles) above Earth.

At this height, the satellite goes into geosynchronous (GEE-O-SIN-CRA-NUSS) orbit. This means it travels at a speed that keeps it over the same spot on Earth while Earth is spinning, too.

The communications satellites in geosynchronous orbit will circle Earth for many years. They will relay telephone calls, television programs, and messages from one part of the globe to the other.

A spinning communications satellite springs out of its protective cover inside the cargo bay. It is programmed to orbit around Earth.

The Stages of a Shuttle Flight

Ten minutes after takeoff, the orbiter is in orbit.

Deorbit begins. Orbiter flies backward; two rocket engines slow orbiter down.

On-board engines shoot the orbiter farther out into space.

Entry. The orbiter becomes red hot as it passes through Earth's atmosphere.

The external tank (ET) separates.

The rocket boosters separate.

Landing

Lift-off.

Getting Ready to Go Home

It's day five, and the plans for this mission have been carried out.

Perhaps you think about seeing your family and friends again. Or sitting down and eating food as you used to. Or seeing trees, or buildings, cars, a pet dog or cat. And not floating around in space.

You've had a chance to do something few people have done so far. Now the crew must get ready to return to Earth. This is the last part of your flight. It is probably not as dangerous as the ascent, but everything must be timed perfectly.

All the instruments are working properly. Each of you has been trained well. You know just what you must do. There are three main steps to bring the orbiter safely back to Earth:

deorbit—stop circling Earth;

entry—leave outer space and enter Earth's atmosphere;

landing—guide the orbiter down onto a runway and stop it.

Before you begin the descent, the cargo bay doors are closed. All things used in orbit must be secured or stowed.

While up in space, the orbiter can get very hot in some spots and very cold in other spots. These uneven temperatures can interfere with the operation of the orbiter as you descend to Earth. So, the night before the descent, the orbiter is put into a steady, gentle roll, like a barbecue. This makes the temperature even all around.

The seats used by the mission specialists and payload specialist during takeoff are put in place for landing. You and the rest of the crew get in your seats and buckle up.

Deorbit

Within one hour you will change from traveling at Mach 26* to a speed slow enough for the orbiter to land—only about 345 kilometers per hour (215 miles per hour)—a little faster than a regular airplane landing.

To *deorbit*, or get out of orbit, you first turn the orbiter around so it flies backward. Then you start the small rocket engines on board and fire them for two to three minutes.

Because the orbiter is flying backward, the firing engines act as a brake. You slow down. As soon as you slow down, you go down, or lose altitude.

*26 times the speed of sound

Now you turn the orbiter back around to fly nose-first again. You will keep losing altitude.

In half an hour, the orbiter drops to an altitude of about 120 kilometers (75 miles). It reaches a thin layer of air—the upper atmosphere of Earth. The orbiter makes its way through the thickening blanket of air that surrounds the planet. You and the crew can feel its drag. You continue to lose speed.

In the next 12 minutes the orbiter will build up tremendous heat. You will be entering Earth's atmosphere. At the same time you will have no contact with anyone on Earth. It will be a difficult and dangerous time.

Entry

Have you ever held your hand outside the window of a moving car? If you hold it straight up, the wind pushes against your hand. If you change the angle so your fingers point into the wind, you feel less push, or pressure.

It's like that for the orbiter. You must keep the nose of the orbiter at just the right angle. The right amount of pressure will slow the craft down. Too much pressure may pull it apart.

With its nose lifted, the orbiter is coming down like a tilted pancake as it moves forward.

The thickness of the atmosphere is due to many tiny particles very close together. The particles are knocked about as the orbiter shoots through them at

The super-high temperatures the orbiter reaches as it passes through Earth's atmosphere turn the protective tiles on the underside red hot. You can see the glow come through the windows inside the cabin.

tremendous speed. The tremendous speed creates tremendous heat.

The high heat changes the tiny particles all around the craft in such a way that messages cannot pass through. You are not able to communicate with Mission Control on Earth during this time. And they cannot reach you.

But you're not really alone up there. Five computers on board the orbiter help you. Four are programmed to carry out the same jobs at just the right instant. If one breaks down, it is ignored and the three others carry on. The fifth computer is a standby if anything goes wrong with all the others.

Computers tell you exactly what your position is, how fast you're going, where you're headed, and so on. During this period, they automatically adjust your position, your altitude, your speed, and other factors all going on at once. Computers make space travel possible.

Twelve minutes have passed. You are 55 kilometers (34 miles) high and coming down about half as fast as when you first hit the atmosphere. You have contact again with the control center on Earth.

In another 20 minutes you will be on the ground.

Landing

There is no fuel to power the orbiter's engines. It lands like a glider. As it nears the runway you can't go around again.

You must figure the correct distance, speed, and angle so you don't miss. The computers give you all the information you need. But now they are not working automatically. You choose the best way to land.

As commander, you know which keys to hit so the computer does its job while you and the pilot do yours. Together, you bring the aircraft down. NASA people call this "fly-by-wire." The commander controls the computer and the computer controls the orbiter.

Touchdown!

Half a minute before you reach the ground, you tilt the nose of the orbiter up sharply. Seconds later the landing gear comes down. Back wheels touch the runway—then comes the nosewheel—*touchdown!* Put on the brakes. The orbiter rolls to a stop.

A ground crew is there to meet you. It takes close to half an hour to cut off switches and shut down systems before leaving the orbiter.

At last, you and the crew climb out of the side hatch. You are back on Earth again!

What else can
the space shuttle do?

The mission on your flight—to deploy communications satellites—is very important. It will probably be repeated often.

Soon, there will be enough satellites in space for us to have information from every part of the globe. The geosynchronous satellites will pick up signals from land, sea, and air. These signals are messages that can be sent to any part of Earth.

Missions are already planned almost to the year 2000. Many will have other purposes. Advanced equipment and space technology make it possible to do interesting, useful—even astonishing—feats in space.

Read about some of them on the next pages.

Extra-Vehicular Activity (EVA)

An astronaut can leave the orbiter and move about in space. Some of the jobs that need to be done outside the orbiter are:
- inspect or photograph payloads;
- change film cassettes;
- clean the television lenses;
- fix wiring;
- transfer cargo;
- perform experiments;
- repair any damage to the outside of the orbiter.

But first, the astronaut must get into a spacesuit. The orbiter carries two spacesuits. Each one allows for six hours of EVA, plus an emergency unit that

Spacewalking (Extra-Vehicle Activity) will be part of many space shuttle missions. Here, the staff at Mission Control in Houston watch an astronaut walk in space, live on TV.

gives the astronaut an extra 30 minutes to get back into the orbiter.

Inside the spacesuit, there is a fruit bar to eat and a straw to sip water near the astronaut's mouth. There is a separate urine container built into the suit.

A backpack on the outside of the spacesuit supplies oxygen for breathing. And a minicomputer in front tells the spacewalker if everything is working right.

Since there's work to be done out there, a portable tool chest is also attached to the front of the spacesuit. The astronaut may have to be a space carpenter, an electrician, a mover, a cameraman, or do some other odd job.

The spacesuit has four parts — pants, top, helmet, and gloves — which are sealed together with connecting rings. This astronaut gets help in putting on the top of his spacesuit. His underwear is called a "spaghetti suit" because it has tubes, like strands of spaghetti, woven into the material. Cool water flows through the tubes, and air ducts provide ventilation to keep his body cool in the airtight spacesuit.

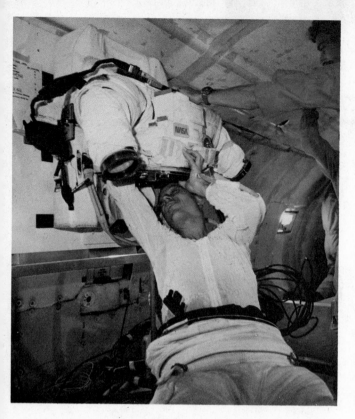

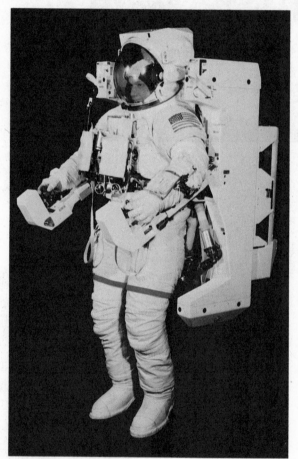

The "Snoopy cap" worn under the helmet has communication wires so that a spacewalker can talk with another spacewalker outside the orbiter and with the crew inside. The cap also keeps the microphones in place.

This astronaut is ready for an EVA mission. His outfit includes light and television equipment, assorted tools, and a Manned Maneuvering Unit (MMU). The MMU is a special backpack that enables the astronaut to propel himself in space. The "arms" of the MMU have hand controls the astronaut uses to start, steer, and stop.

Spacelab

Spacelab fits in the cargo bay. It is a place to do many kinds of experiments. They will include testing humans, plants, animals, and minerals to see how they are affected by microgravity.

New products and medicines will probably be created that will improve life on Earth. Astronomers and astrophysicists will have a "front seat" to look at the stars, the planets, and the universe.

Spacelab is a very important part of NASA's Space Transportation System. It was developed by the European Space Agency (ESA) and paid for by ten countries in Europe. European scientists will also be on board for some of the missions.

The "crew module" is the part of Spacelab where scientists work. In this drawing, you can see inside the module. The real module is completely enclosed.

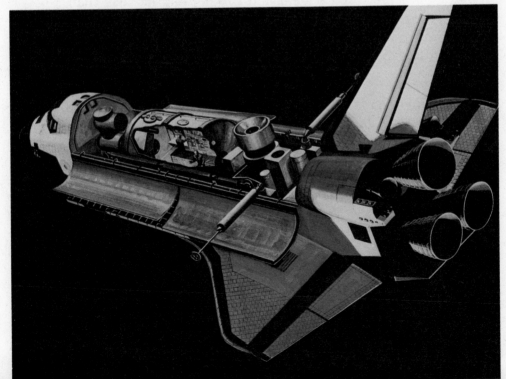

Space Telescope

Telescopes on the ground have a limited view because Earth's atmosphere interferes. By taking a powerful telescope far above the atmosphere we can get a much clearer view of what is in deep space.

The Space Telescope gives astronomers a much better idea of how the universe began. It also helps them understand what changes will probably occur in the future. We will learn more about our solar system, quasars, pulsars, black holes, and extra-terrestrial life. We will probably learn things we know nothing about yet.

"Getaway Specials"

If there is room, the orbiter will take up small payloads for individuals. These "Getaway Specials" cost between $3,000 and $10,000—a lot less than the regular payload.

A "Getaway Special" must have a useful purpose, weigh less than 91 kilograms (200 pounds), and be small enough to fit into a cannister about the size and shape of a large garbage can. It must not use much electrical power or need special attention, except to be turned on or off.

More than 300 people from the United States and many other countries have already signed up for a chance to send up their space ideas.

Part of the "Getaway Specials" program is a contest held by NASA and the National Science Teachers Association. Any student who develops a space science experiment may enter the contest. The winners' experiments are taken up on the shuttle.

Long Duration Exposure Facility

This is a long cylinder with 76 shallow trays which hold a variety of objects and materials. The cylinder is placed in orbit and left there for half a year or more.

A Space Exposure Facility

Tracking and Data Relay Satellites

Before the Tracking and Data Relay Satellites, many stations on Earth tried to keep track of spacecraft in low orbits. But they could make contact only for short periods.

The Space Transportation System now has three Tracking and Data Relay Satellites. Two will be placed in geosynchronous orbit—one over the Pacific Ocean, the other over the Atlantic Ocean. The third is a backup.

These satellites will receive signals from low-orbiting spacecraft most of the time.

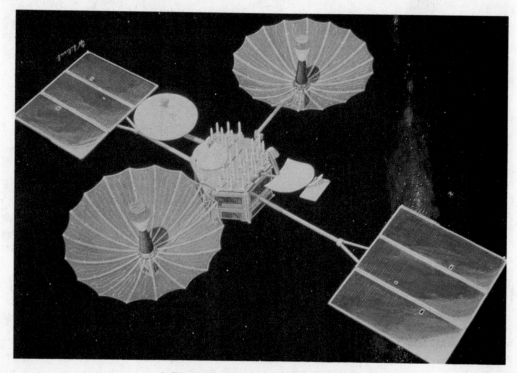

A Tracking and Data Relay Satellite

The Space Transportation System (STS)

The space shuttle is the first vehicle created by humans that can carry them into space, keep them safely there, bring them back to Earth, and be used again and again.

The shuttle's capability to do this means that the cost of such a vehicle can be kept down. (Imagine what it would cost if you had to throw away a bicycle and build a new one every time you used it!)

Money is also saved by making many parts a standard size that can connect with other parts. Such designs are called modules. A new module can replace a damaged or old one. Different combinations of modules make use of the shuttle in various ways.

Another way to make the shuttle pay is to charge for carrying cargo—the payload.

These possibilities led to the development of the Space Transportation System—a complete Earth-space connection.

STS has two main purposes:
- to be able to go back and forth into space often and at low cost;
- to make use of space for the benefit of people on Earth.

STS includes the shuttle, with its tank, rocket boosters, and orbiter. There will be a fleet of at least four orbiters, named after old-time explorer ships: *Columbia, Challenger, Discovery,* and *Atlantis.*

STS also includes:

- Spacelab;
- the manipulator arm;
- rockets that shoot payloads into geosynchronous orbits or to other planets;
- a complex computer system;
- a communications network for ground and space;
- launch sites;
- service facilities to build and repair equipment;
- cargo handling;
- control centers and offices.

Of all the branches of STS, the most important are the people—men and women whose knowledge and work make the Space Transportation System possible. You may be among them one day.

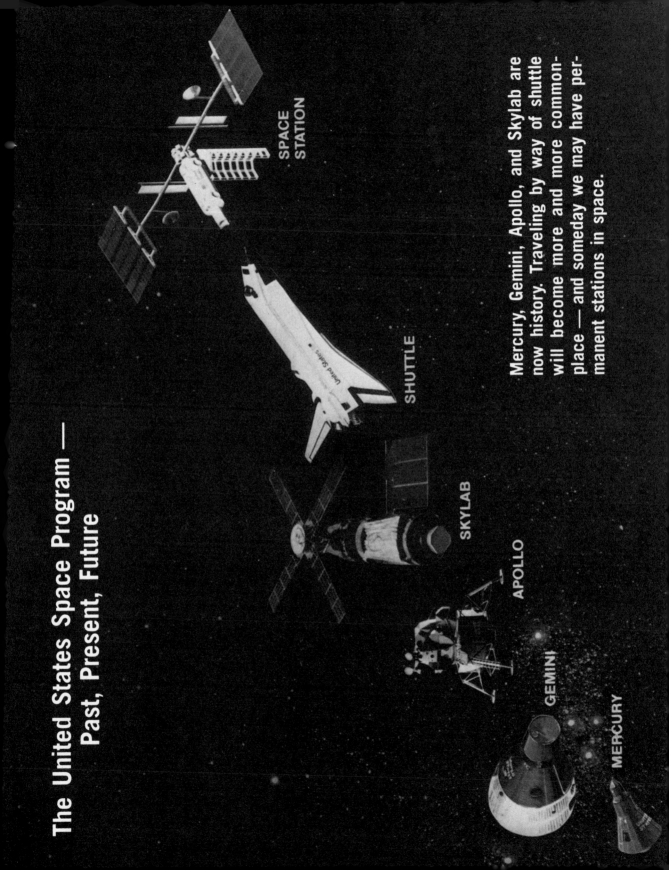

The United States Space Program — Past, Present, Future

SPACE STATION

SHUTTLE

SKYLAB

APOLLO

GEMINI

MERCURY

Mercury, Gemini, Apollo, and Skylab are now history. Traveling by way of shuttle will become more and more common-place — and someday we may have per-manent stations in space.

A note from the author
about the uses of space technology

It would be difficult to list the many uses of space that benefit people on Earth.

Some are a direct result of what the Space Transportation System does. Some are a result of the technology. Those uses are called "spin-offs," because the ability to do one task often leads to the ability to do another.

These are some of the uses of space that already exist:

Communications—A satellite system covers the globe. "Live via satellite" brings into our homes news and sports events as they happen in some other part of the planet.

We can exchange telephone calls and do business across continents.

Educational programs and medical instructions can be sent to villages that would otherwise never be reached.

Rescue operations for lost aircraft and ships in trouble, as well as directing air traffic over the oceans, are now possible.

Emergency communications during disasters, such as the volcanic eruption of Mt. St. Helens, help save lives.

Weather observations—Photos from weather satellites are part of our daily lives. We know whether to wear a heavy coat, take an umbrella, get out the snow shovel or a bathing suit.

This photo taken from space shows a part of the Atlantic Ocean called Great Bahama Bank. The dark blue area indicates an underwater cliff one mile deep. The wavy lines are probably coral.

Early forecasts of hurricanes, blizzards, floods, and other bad weather give people a chance to seek shelter and save some belongings.

Farmers use forecasts to decide when to plant, irrigate, fertilize, or spread insecticides.

Checking Earth's natural resources—Measurements taken from the orbiter or from satellites tell us details about our mountains, valleys, rivers, lakes, and other kinds of surfaces on our planet.

Geologists can now get information on what lies beneath the surfaces—what minerals to mine or petroleum to find, which huge areas of land are moving slightly, where there may be an earthquake, and so on.

Photos and instruments show air pollution on a world-wide scale.

The growth of timber or diseases of plant life can be monitored. Forest fires can be detected early.

Oceanography—Movement of icebergs can be charted to help ships at sea.

Currents, waves, surface winds affect our fishing industry. Photos from space give information about where algae and plankton that fish feed on are located. Fishermen can catch fish there. That adds to the food people eat.

Medicine and health care—New equipment for scanning diseases and illnesses has come out of space technology. These instruments help doctors treat patients.

Microgravity is producing new drugs and medications that could not be made on Earth.

Materials—Fireproof fabrics are now available for clothes and home use. Sports clothes that are light and comfortable have also been developed.

Food—New, simple ways of preparing food for the elderly, based on what astronauts eat, are another result of the space program.

Astronomy—We can be much more thorough in our exploration of the solar system and even other star systems. We can go much farther and see much more than ever before.

National security—Countries will use space technology for defense.

There is no limit to what we can achieve. We will be using more and more of the sun's energy to accomplish jobs on Earth.

We will probably have a space station in orbit one day where people can stay for long periods of time. Their work and research should bring us new benefits.

Many people believe that someday there will be a new place to live—a hometown in space! Meanwhile, more and more people on Earth will become space travelers.